DISCARDED

The Library of the Thirteen Colonies and the Lost Colony™

The Colony of South Carolina

Susan Whitehurst

The Rosen Publishing Group's
PowerKids Press™
New York

For Whitney

Published in 2000 by The Rosen Publishing Group, Inc.
29 East 21st Street, New York, NY 10010

Copyright © 2000 by The Rosen Publishing Group, Inc.

All rights reserved. No part of this book may be reproduced in any form without permission in writing from the publisher, except by a reviewer.

Photo Credits: Cover and title page, pp. 1, 8, 11, 16, 20 © North Wind Pictures; pp. 7, 19 © Stock Montage; p. 13 © The Image Works; p. 14, 15 © Super Stock; p. 4, 12, 15 © The Granger Collection; p. 22 © Corbis-Bettman.

First Edition

Book Design: Andrea Levy

Whitehurst, Susan.
    The Colony of South Carolina / by Susan Whitehurst.
        p.   cm. — (The library of the thirteen colonies and the Lost Colony)
    Includes index.
    Summary: Introduces important people and events in the history of South Carolina from colonization to statehood.
    ISBN 0-8239-5486-2
    1. South Carolina—History—Colonial period, ca. 1600-1775 Juvenile literature. 2. South Carolina—History—1775-1865 Juvenile literature. [1. South Carolina—History—Colonial period, ca. 1600–1775. 2. South Carolina—History—1775-1865.]   I. Title. II. Series.
    F272.W57 1999
    975.7'02—dc21   99-14963
                                                                                                              CIP

Manufactured in the United States of America

Contents

Founding Carolina

In the 1500s, people started to come from Europe to live in America. They settled in **colonies** that would later become the United States. Spain and France each started a colony in the area that is now South Carolina, but both colonies failed. King Charles of England became interested in this land and the area that is now North Carolina in 1629. He named the property Carolana, or "Land of Charles," after himself. In 1663, the King's son, King Charles II, changed the spelling to Carolina. He gave the land to eight family friends as a gift. These eight Englishmen became the **Lords Proprietors** of Carolina.

The English already had more than 12 colonies in America by the time South Carolina was settled in 1669.

King Charles of England claimed the colony of Carolana and named it after himself.

Settlers in Charles Town

In 1669, the Lords Proprietors sent 100 people from England to settle in South Carolina. After living through storms and two ship wrecks, the colonists arrived at Albemarle Point in May 1670. There they began the first settlement, called

The Charleston colonists marked where streets would go before they built the city. This was a new idea in the colonies. Most towns went up without plans.

Charles Town, later shortened to Charleston. They built homes, shops, and a port for ships. More people came to Charleston from England. Land was cheap, and people of any religion were welcome. Colonists planted corn and potatoes, but the land was swampy and their crops didn't grow well. The colonists might have starved if it were not for shipments of food they got from England and trade with nearby Indians.

When settlers first arrived in Charleston, they had no place to live, so they built temporary shelters. ▶

Ruling South Carolina

The northern and southern parts of Carolina were very different. In 1712, North and South Carolina became separate colonies. South Carolina's Lords Proprietors stayed in England and sent governors to rule the colony. To make money, the lords charged settlers rent to live there. The governors they sent cheated the colonists and kept raising their rents. They didn't help the colony during wars with the Tuscarora and Yamasee Indians or protect the colony from pirates. Finally, in 1719, the colonists rebelled against the lords and threw the governor out of office. They sent a messenger to England to ask the new king, King George, to make South Carolina a royal colony so that it could be ruled and protected by him. King George agreed.

When South Carolina colonists went to war with the Tuscarora Indians, their English governor did not help them.

Rice and Indigo

South Carolina's first settlers weren't sure how they would make money. Farming had not been very successful. Colonists began capturing Native Americans and selling them as slaves to people in other colonies and in the West Indian islands. The colonists knew they would have to find a better way to make money. By the early 1700s, they'd discovered that rice grew well in the swampy land, and **indigo** could be planted behind the **rice paddies**. Rice and indigo made the farmers rich. To do the hard work on the large **plantations**, colonists had black slaves shipped from Africa. By the early 1700s, there were more black slaves than white colonists in South Carolina.

Colonists kept having problems growing indigo until a teenager, Eliza Pinckney, began experimenting and found better ways to grow the crop in 1744.

African slaves were used instead of Native Americans because they were far from home and had nowhere to go if they ran away. Indian slaves ran away and returned to their villages.

Life in Charleston

By 1760, Charleston was one of the richest towns in all the colonies. Farmers brought rice and indigo to Charleston Harbor to be shipped out on the hundreds of ships that docked there. The town had a newspaper, a theater, a large bookstore, horse races, and musical concerts. White plantation owners kept slaves who cleaned their homes, cooked their meals, and drove them around in fancy carriages. Charleston was a fine place to live if you were a white colonist. Charleston was a hard place to live, though, if you were black. Half of the slaves who came to the colonies came through Charleston Harbor.

Slaves who worked in people's homes often had a better life than slaves who worked in the fields, but they were not free and had no legal rights.

Life as a Slave

By the late 1700s, 60,000 slaves lived in South Carolina. Most had been captured in Africa, shipped to Charleston Harbor, and sold. Families were often separated when mothers, fathers, and children were bought by different plantation owners. Slaves worked long hours in the rice paddies and indigo fields. It was against the law to teach a slave to read or write, because slave owners were afraid that educated slaves would rebel. Plantation owners did not want slaves to keep their African cultures, either. Slaves learned to mix some of their African traditions with their new way of life. In South Carolina, slaves made a new language, called Gullah, that mixed English with their African languages. This was one way that slaves kept their African identity.

At slave auctions like this one, husbands and wives, brothers and sisters, and parents and children were separated, never to see one another again. ▶

Low Country and Up Country

The colonists thought of South Carolina as being divided into Low Country and Up Country. The most important towns (Charleston, Georgetown, and Beaufort) and the rich plantations were in the Low Country by the coast. However, most of the people of South Carolina lived in Up Country. They were **frontier** people, who owned few slaves. The frontier families lived in log cabins, made clothes out of **buckskin**, and hunted and farmed for their food. When a new family moved nearby, their neighbors would all get together to help them build a cabin. After the cabin was finished, people would celebrate by having a shooting contest and dancing to **fiddle** music.

◄ *The women of an Up Country frontier community cook while the men help a new neighbor build a cabin.*

17

Stamps and Tea

In the 1760s, England decided to raise money by **taxing** the colonists. The English Stamp Act of 1765 taxed newspapers and legal papers. The taxes made the colonists angry, and they refused to pay them. They didn't think it was fair that they had no Colonial **representatives** in the English government to vote for the laws. The colonists of Charleston hung a dummy of an English tax collector from a tree to scare anyone who tried to collect the taxes. Then the English taxed tea. The colonists in South Carolina got so mad they dumped three shiploads of tea into Charleston Harbor, just like the settlers in Boston had done during the famous Boston Tea Party.

This colonist attacks a tax collector when he tries to collect money from her. ▶

The Revolutionary War

Colonial leaders met in Philadelphia in 1774 to decide what should be done. They asked the king to stop taxing the colonies, but he refused. Then on April 19, 1775, in Lexington, Massachusetts, colonists and British soldiers began shooting at one another. The American Revolutionary War had begun.

The English wanted to control the important harbor at Charleston. In 1776, they sent 11 warships to capture the town. The colonists built a fort of **palmetto tree** logs to protect Charleston. The English fired cannonballs at the fort, but the fort didn't fall. The wood of the palmetto is so soft that the cannonballs sank into the logs without destroying the fort. After 12 hours of fighting, the English gave up. Charleston was saved.

◀ *The Charleston colonists protected their city by firing at British ships out at sea.*

A New State

Over 100 battles were fought in South Carolina during the Revolutionary War. Eight years later, the Americans won the Revolutionary War. The colonies joined to become a new nation.

More than 150 years after King Charles had claimed the colony and named it Carolana, South Carolina approved the U.S. Constitution and became the eighth state. In honor of the way that the palmetto tree had helped the colony, it was named the state tree. The palmetto is now shown on the state flag of the beautiful and proud state of South Carolina.

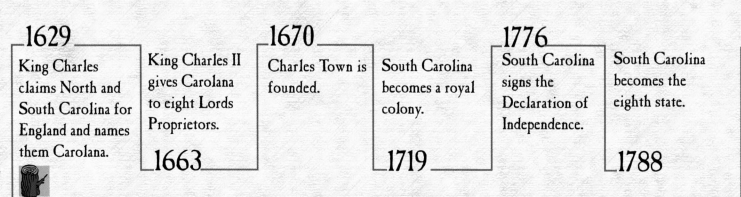

1629		1670		1776	
King Charles claims North and South Carolina for England and names them Carolana.	King Charles II gives Carolana to eight Lords Proprietors.	Charles Town is founded.	South Carolina becomes a royal colony.	South Carolina signs the Declaration of Independence.	South Carolina becomes the eighth state.
	1663		1719		1788

Glossary

buckskin (BUHK-skin) Leather made from the skin of a deer.

colonies (KAH-luh-neez) Areas in a new country where a large group of people move who are still ruled by the leaders and laws of their old country.

fiddle (FIH-dul) A violin.

frontier (frun-TEER) The edge of a settled country, where the wilderness begins.

indigo (IN-dih-go) A plant that can be used to make blue dye.

Lords Proprietors (LORDS pruh-PRY-uh-turz) People who were given a colony for which they made the laws and who could give or sell the land to others.

palmetto tree (pahl-MEH-toh TREE) A low palm tree with soft wood and fan-like leaves.

plantations (plan-TAY-shun) A very large farm where crops like tobacco and cotton were grown. Many plantation owners used slaves to work these farms.

representatives (reh-prih-zen-TAY-shun) When people are elected to the government to do what the voters want them to do.

rice paddies (RYS PA-deez) Wet areas of land where rice is grown.

taxing (TAK-sing) When the government collects money from people to help pay for public services.

Index

Web Sites:

You can learn more about Colonial South Carolina on the Internet.
Check out this Web site:
http://www.geocities.com/Athens/Oracle/5650/southcarolina.htm